THE NEW MID...
REGIME STABILITY IN SAUDI ARABIA

HARVARD
MIDDLE·EAST·PAPERS
MODERN SERIES: NUMBER THREE

MARK HELLER AND NADAV SAFRAN

THE NEW MIDDLE CLASS AND REGIME STABILITY IN SAUDI ARABIA

CENTER FOR MIDDLE EASTERN STUDIES • HARVARD UNIVERSITY
1737 CAMBRIDGE STREET • CAMBRIDGE • MASSACHUSETTS • 02138

ISBN 0-932885-00-4

Library of Congress Catalog Card Number 85-47504
© 1985 President and Fellows of Harvard College
    Center for Middle Eastern Studies

Printed in the United States of America

HARVARD MIDDLE EAST PAPERS

The Harvard Middle East Papers are occasional publications of the Center for Middle Eastern Studies at Harvard University. The Middle East Papers deal with all branches of social and cultural inquiry about the area reaching from Egypt to Pakistan and from Turkey to southern Arabia. They deal with a single topic at a length between that of an article and a book. The Classical Series includes research on topics to about the year 1800; the Modern Series includes research on topics since then. Papers that help illuminate policy are particularly welcome.

Although the Papers are intended primarily as a forum for work done under Center auspices, we welcome submissions from other sources.

Each paper represents the views of the author alone and not necessarily those of the Center for Middle Eastern Studies.

Center for Middle Eastern Studies
Harvard University
Nadav Safran, *Director*

Modern Series Editorial Committee
Daniel Pipes, *Chair*
Lisa Anderson, Thomas Barfield, Bernard Cooperman

HARVARD MIDDLE EAST PAPERS
MODERN SERIES

When the aptitude to command and to exercise political control is no longer the sole possession of the legal rulers but has become common enough among other people; when outside the ruling class another class has formed which finds itself deprived of power though it does have the capacity to share in the responsibilities of government—then that [ruling class] has become an obstacle in the path of an elemental force and must, by one way or another, go.
                                                              —Gaetano Mosca

THE AUTHORS

Mark Heller received his Ph.D. in political science from Harvard University in 1976 and was a Visiting Scholar at Harvard's Center for International Affairs in 1982–83. His publications include a monograph entitled *The Iran-Iraq War: Implications for Third Parties* (Harvard CFIA and Tel Aviv University's Jaffee Center for Strategic Studies).

Nadav Safran is Murray A. Albertson Professor of Middle Eastern Studies and Director of the Center for Middle Eastern Studies at Harvard University. His extensive writings on the Middle East include the forthcoming *Saudi Arabia: The Ceaseless Quest for Security* (Harvard University Press).

ABSTRACT

Historically, modernization attempts by traditional regimes have produced a new middle class that, after attaining a certain level of development, has turned against the regime in moments of crises.

In Saudi Arabia, a new middle class has reached or is about to reach this critical stage of evolution. Although certain seemingly exceptional conditions exist in that country, these do not nullify the applicability to it of the historical "rule."

Consequently, regime-destabilizing behavior and action by new middle class elements in the years ahead will depend on the occurrence of a trigger crisis. The chances of a crisis within the next ten years are better than even.

CONTENTS

TABLES

1. INTRODUCTION

The modern history of the Middle East is testimony to the fragility of traditional regimes. Since World War II, monarchies have been overthrown in Egypt, Iraq, Yemen, Libya, and Iran and have been sorely tested in Jordan and Morocco. In the same period, the traditional elite in Syria, though it ruled on republican lines, was also brought down, and the regime in Lebanon has survived only as a legal fiction.

The instability and upheaval that characterize Middle Eastern politics have many causes—ethnic and religious tensions, inter-state conflict, ideological antagonisms—but one major source is undoubtedly rapid social change. The articulators and organizers of political discontent have typically belonged to social formations of relatively recent origin as have those—usually politicized, middle grade army officers—who actually carried out the coups d'état. These agents of change come from a new middle class created by traditional rulers intent on strengthening their societies through selective modernization measures. Once that class attains a certain level of development, it tends to press for modernization beyond the point intended by the rulers. The accumulating tension is often ignited by a major failure of the regime, especially in the defense sphere, and the explosion frequently leads to a seizure of power by the military element of the new middle class. The military-led regimes tend to espouse extremist populist doctrines and policies.

The Arabian Peninsula, excepting the special case of the Yemens, has not yet undergone this experience, perhaps because rapid modernization in this part of the region began much later. (North Yemen underwent a military coup in 1962 even though the new middle class was still embryonic because of outside instigation. In South Yemen, leftist nationalist elements that developed in the "hothouse" of Aden city captured the anti-British movement and imposed their rule on the rest of the country.) In recent years, however, massive oil revenues have stimulated a social and economic transformation of unprecedented speed and intensity. The potential implications of this transformation in Saudi Arabia are of special concern, not only because that country is the world's largest oil exporter but also because Saudi Arabia's fate will certainly determine that of the other principalities on the periphery of the peninsula.

This study will present a conceptual model of the middle class and a brief review of its emergence as a universal phenomenon, followed by a description of its historical and prospective growth in Saudi Arabia. The relationship between the new middle class and the monarchy will be analyzed next in the context of challenges the regime is likely to encounter.

The main conclusion of the study is that a new middle class has already emerged as a pivotal social formation in Saudi Arabia. This class may have no vested interest in the short term in subverting or destroying the present Saudi regime. In the longer run, serious contradictions between the new middle class and the regime are likely to arise, and the regime's ability to deal with them will be impaired, perhaps fatally, if a major crisis occurs as a result of disunity in the royal family, a major economic setback, or a dramatic military embarrassment. There is a strong probability that some such crisis will erupt in the coming decade, and if it does, the new middle class may very well turn decisively against the regime.

2. THE NEW MIDDLE CLASS IN HISTORICAL PERSPECTIVE

Perhaps the greatest problem facing traditional regimes is the containment of the political consequences of social and economic modernization. Modern economic activities and changing relations with the outside world produce new economic roles and generate demands for new skills. Those who emerge to fulfill these roles stand outside the traditional pattern of social stratification and are often alienated from the traditional political order, to the point where they appear to have appropriated the function of opposition. One student of political development has identified these people by typical occupation—lawyers and doctors, teachers and journalists, modern bureaucrats and army officers, and those unemployed in jails, coffee houses, or universities.[1] In colonial societies they have been called "marginal men" because they straddled the worlds of traditional native society and modern European society but belonged to neither.[2] In post-colonial societies, or in those that have never experienced direct European rule, they can be categorized as the new middle class.

The term class, however, is something of a misnomer, at least in the Marxian sense of relation to the means of production. The groups in question own neither land nor capital. The professionals do "own" their means of production, usually consisting of their own labor; but unlike the typical bourgeoisie, they are not an employing class. The others are employees, but they sell their labor to state institutions rather than directly to other classes. Although the term stratum might convey a more precise notion of their collective character, they do constitute a distinct social formation because of two other peculiar attributes. The first is that they did not exist in the traditional order. As the product of the modernization process, they are not heirs to any traditional corporate identity or loyalty. The second definitional characteristic is possession of modern, secular education—knowledge, skills, techniques, and training in sciences or technologies imported from the Western world. This new type of education is their unique asset and the basis for their claim to status, income, and sometimes power.

The groups that make up this new middle class—bureaucrats, army officers, teachers of secular subjects, and self-employed modern professionals—sometimes appear to be inevitably hostile to the traditional order. In fact, the historical role of the new middle class has varied with

3

time stage, the conditions of that class's evolution, and the performance of the traditional regime.

In Western societies, the groups we call new middle class emerge as by-products of autochthonous economic development. In this "classical" pattern, members of these groups are linked to private enterprises as well as to the state, usually a centralizing monarch, and are therefore identified with both political elites and bourgeois counter-elites. Lacking a distinct corporate character, they have been found on both sides of the barricades in the great social confrontations and political revolutions of early modern Europe.

In most developing societies, by contrast, the new middle class is a product of modernization prompted solely by state initiative or the presence of a colonial occupier. State initiative, often described as defensive modernization, is the response of traditional regimes threatened by expanding Western power and culture. In countries as remote from one another as Russia and Mexico, the Ottoman Empire and Japan, rulers have sought to resist the undeniable strength of Britain, France, and the United States by emulating the apparent sources of Western superiority—economic, technological, and organizational modernity. In order to staff a centralized administration, to implement land reform and industrialization, and, most important, to build up and command effective armies and navies, these regimes recruit or encourage promising individuals with traditional education to acquire Western knowledge and skills. In short, traditional regimes create a new middle class to work with and for them.

This class quickly evolves as a distinct entity associated with the modernization effort, but its relationship with the regime that brings it into existence changes over time and passes through several stages. In the first stage, the new middle class has ample scope to apply its training and skills to the implementation of reforms initiated by the ruling elite. At a subsequent stage, the roles of new middle class and regime are reversed; the former, because of momentum and intra-bureaucratic competition, assumes a leading role in advocating and promoting accelerated development, which the ruling elite then endorses and promulgates.

At some point in the process, however, the modernizing endeavor of the new middle class begins to encroach upon the most sensitive areas of the regime, such as the privileges of the ruler, the basis of the political order, and the religious and cultural underpinnings of both. The threatened regime, never unreservedly committed to modernization, resists, hesitates, and prevaricates, and consequently alienates the new middle class, for whom modernization has, at this stage, become an end in itself, dictated by its ethos and world outlook.

It is possible for the strain between new middle class and traditional ruler to persist for a considerable length of time without serious danger to the political order because the new middle class usually lacks the inherent solidarity to act as a revolutionary class. However, if the state is confronted with a major crisis and found wanting, the alienated new middle class is often galvanized to act. In such circumstances, the middle class tends to abandon its creator, the traditional regime, and to transfer its allegiance to revolutionary forces who carry out a coup and promise a truly effective modernization program.

The pattern outlined here describes the experiences of many, though not all, defensive modernizers; it is a particularly apt summary of the stages through which the Ottoman Empire passed in its last century, which began with the Tanzimat and ended with the secular republicanism of Mustafa Kemal Ataturk.

The second process by which the new middle class is created involves an even more direct and intrusive foreign role. Foreign occupation of a traditional society, because of the administrative and economic modernization stimulated by the occupation, usually has a profound, if sometimes unintended, impact on the latter's social and cultural structures. Even if the imperial powers are interested only in the economic exploitation of their outlying possessions, the development of extractive industries and the commercialization of agriculture result in new skills, occupations, and perspectives among the local population. Furthermore, foreign occupiers are compelled to rely to some extent on indigenous elements to provide information, implement policies, maintain order, and legitimize the occupier's role. These elements are usually equipped with some modern knowledge or technical training and co-opted into the middle ranks of the administrative, judicial, or military bureaucracies. Colonial powers with a self-imposed "civilizing mission" also provide higher education for a select few, thus creating a rudimentary corps of native professionals. In this way, European rule produces new middle classes in traditional societies (while simultaneously discrediting the old elites).

This new middle class may initially embrace the cause of modernization and identify with the imperial/colonial power that brings it into being, but eventually it turns against the foreign rulers because it concludes that they, like native defensive modernizers, are not wholehearted in their commitment to modernization. More critically, the new middle class usually comes to espouse a fervent nationalism, unmitigated by other collective identities or countervailing interests. The traditional elites, for instance, may be politically dispossessed by the institution of foreign rule, but their economic and cultural preeminence is frequently preserved or even enhanced. Modern new classes of large landowners or capitalists may emerge under foreign occupation and initiate movements for self-rule or independence, but because they actually owe their enrichment to foreign rule, they tend to be ambivalent in their nationalist commitment. The new middle class has no such restraints, and regardless of the origin of the nationalist movement, that class therefore usually assumes an increasingly prominent role in the movement and pushes it in more radical directions. If independence is achieved while traditional or landowner-capitalist forces still dominate the movement, their inclination to maintain external ties that serve their interests, that is, to facilitate a "neo-colonialist" relationship, alienates the radicalized new middle class and often leads to a military coup in the early post-independence period.

The typical behavior of the new middle class can therefore be summarized as follows:

1. The new middle class is a creation of defensive-modernizer or foreign-imperial regimes.

2. The new middle class, by its very nature, has no intrinsic collective interest, economic or ideological, in the preservation of the regime.

3. Its attitude toward defensive modernizers is dialectical, that is, it differs at various stages in its evolution. The new middle class is initially associated with, and follows the lead of, the traditional regime that brings it into being. At a subsequent stage, the new middle class presses to move more vigorously along the path of modernization and the regime follows, though with increasing misgivings. In the third stage, new middle class demands encroach on the most sensitive values of the traditional regime and serious strains develop, but as long as defensive modernization appears to be relatively successful, the new middle class either remains loyal to the regime or mutes its opposition. If the inadequacy of the modernization effort is exposed, as it often is (most dramatically, because of military defeat), important elements of the new middle class defect to revolutionary forces and, in a fourth stage of evolution, help bring about the destruction of the old order.

4. Its attitude toward imperial or colonial progenitors is almost invariably hostile, for nationalist reasons, and the new middle class tends to push nationalism in radical directions, either before independence, if other classes show signs of compromise, or after independence, if native rulers are insufficiently resistant to "neo-colonial" relations with the West.

3. THE GROWTH OF THE NEW MIDDLE CLASS IN SAUDI ARABIA

In most respects, Saudi experience has resembled the defensive modernization pattern of social change. The new Saudi middle class is the creature of a traditional monarchy bent on maintaining the religious, cultural, and political foundations of its rule while promoting a thoroughgoing economic and infrastructural transformation of the kingdom. The regime believes as a matter of faith that this transformation is consistent with traditional values and can even help entrench them.

The picture is somewhat complicated, however, by the intrusion of elements from the second process of social modernization—foreign occupation. Saudi Arabia has never undergone direct foreign rule, but it was exposed to a large foreign presence in connection with the development of the oil industry. The American oil companies, by building a modern sector in a primitive economy, created part of the new Saudi middle class and also provided the massive revenues that made regime-directed modernization both possible and necessary. By their very presence they also constituted a focus of nationalist resentment. Moreover, Saudi Arabia has been part of a larger Arab collectivity in which radical pan-Arab nationalism, often directed against the United States, has been a pervasive force.

The theory of Arab nationalism postulates the existence of a national identity transcending local patriotism and the sovereignty of individual Arab states. This theory has encouraged, and legitimized, the efforts of radical leaders in other Arab capitals, acting in the name of Arab unity, to support dissident forces inside Saudi Arabia and to undermine a Saudi regime vulnerable, despite its undeniably indigenous origins, to charges of neo-colonialist ties and insufficient pan-Arab enthusiasm. To ensure the allegiance, even if only passive, of the new middle class, the Saudi rulers must therefore be aware not only of the instrumental test of defensive modernizers (the need to acquire general effectiveness through modernization and especially the capacity to preserve the state's political sovereignty) but also of the nationalist test of post-colonial regimes (the need to protect society against the alleged political, economic, and cultural machinations of predatory Western powers). Both these tests will become increasingly arduous as the new middle class assumes a larger and more central role in Saudi affairs.

7

In contrast to the traditional image of Saudi society, the Saudi state, like others in the Middle East, is of relatively recent origin. The Saudi Arab Kingdom in its present configuration did not exist before the conquest of the Hijaz in 1925 by Abd al-Aziz ibn Abd al-Rahman Al Faisal Al Saud (r. 1902–53). The country's name was not officially adopted until 1932, and formal administrative unity was decreed only in 1953. The kingdom owes its existence to the political and military leadership of Abd al-Aziz, but its prosperity and importance to the rest of the world are a function of oil, which was discovered in the late 1930s and exported in substantial quantities after the Second World War.

The revenues derived from oil exports were initially modest; in the 1950s Saudi Arabia was still a recipient of American economic aid, and until the 1960s the budget was seldom balanced. The revenues that accrued were administered in a haphazard fashion, largely because the state lacked even the rudiments of a functioning bureaucratic apparatus. A council of ministers was not convened until 1954; no distinction was made between the public treasury and the privy purse of the king; and the ineffectiveness and conspicuous consumption of the royal family that characterized much of the reign of Saud ibn Abd al-Aziz (r. 1953–64) resulted in serious domestic and external weakness. Although some within the royal family felt that political liberalization might best correct these weaknesses, the dominant response to pressure for change was centralization and a commitment to serious development programs, which were intended to make the administration more effective, produce a more tolerable distribution of wealth, and build up military and para-military forces capable of protecting the regime against potential foreign and domestic threats. This effort was directed by Saud's brother, Faisal ibn Abd al-Aziz, who was, at the insistence of the senior princes, made prime minister from 1958 to 1960 and again from 1962 to 1964, when the hapless King Saud was finally forced to abdicate in his favor.

Before Faisal's accession to the throne, Saudi Arabia was still a relatively poor country. Annual government revenues barely exceeded $500 million, a significant proportion of which was accounted for by non-oil sources, especially the *hajj* (annual Muslim pilgrimage to Mecca). The noticeable rise in oil income that took place in the late 1960s almost doubled government revenues before the end of the decade and permitted the sustained development drive to begin.[3] Outlays in those years naturally pale in comparison with the dramatic changes after 1973 (see table 1), but directed modernization can nevertheless be dated from that period and is reflected in the growth of the new middle class.

Table 1. Saudi oil revenues, 1965–82 ($ billion)

Year	Revenue
1965	0.7
1970	1.2
1971	1.9
1972	2.7
1973	4.3
1974	22.6
1975	25.7
1976	30.8
1977	36.5
1978	32.2
1979	48.4
1980	84.5
1981	102.1
1982	70.5

Source: Ministry of Petroleum and Natural Resources, *Petroleum Statistical Bulletin*, no. 13, 1982, p. 14.

The modernization drive entailed the expansion of the state bureaucracy (in order to implement a host of economic and public welfare projects), the security forces (in order to safeguard the country and the regime), and the educational system (in order to train the literate manpower needed by the other two institutions). These three sectors provided the main components of the new Saudi middle class: middle and upper grade civil servants (grades 7 through 15 in the Saudi classification), whose skill levels and status suggest a middle class orientation; the officer corps of the various security apparatuses; and teachers of modern subjects. To these should ideally be added upper level employees in the private sector and independent practitioners of the free professions. Specific data on these latter groups, however, have proved to be scarce, and the general information available suggests that the number of Saudi nationals involved is rather small.

Data on the size and growth of the new middle class, in the sense just defined, are presented in table 2, which includes projections for 1985.

Table 2. The new middle class in Saudi Arabia, 1965–85

Size and growth of main component groups (Saudi nationals only, rounded to nearest hundred)

Group	1965	1970	1975	1980	1985
Civil servants[a]	3,600	6,000	18,100	40,700	56,800
(% increase)		(67)	(202)	(125)	(40)
Military officers[b]	5,600[c]	6,000	7,000	7,400	11,100
(% increase)		(7)	(17)	(6)	(50)
Teachers[d]	5,700	10,200	22,200	38,000	45,300
(% increase)		(79)	(118)	(71)	(19)
Total	14,900	22,200	47,300	86,200	113,200
(% increase)		(49)	(113)	(82)	(31)

a. Grades 7–15. Figures are derived from Kingdom of Saudi Arabia, *Statistical Yearbook* (various years). See app. A for an explanation of methods.

b. Assumed to be 10 percent of combined strength of regular armed forces and National Guard. Figures are derived from the International Institute of Strategic Studies, *The Military Balance* (various years). See app. B for an explanation of methods.

c. Figure for 1967.

d. Figures are derived from Kingdom of Saudi Arabia, *Statistical Yearbook* (various years). See app. C for an explanation of methods.

As is clear from the figures presented here, the new middle class in Saudi Arabia has grown dramatically, in absolute numbers, in a short period of time. Its relative weight, as represented by its percentage of the labor force, has grown even more impressively. Our calculations, summarized in table 3, show that the three main component groups of the new middle class accounted for a mere 2.1 percent of the labor force of Saudi nationals in 1966. By 1980 this figure had grown to 7.2 percent. By 1985 it is projected to reach at least 8.1 percent.

Table 3. The new middle class as a percentage of Saudi labor force

	1965	1975	1980	1985
Labor force[a]	712,800[b]	1,026,400	1,190,000	1,379,500
New middle class[c]	14,900	47,300	86,200	113,200
New middle class as % of labor force	2.1	4.6	7.2	8.1

a. Numbers are rounded to the nearest hundred. Figures are derived from J. S. Birks and C. A. Sinclair, *Arab Manpower* (London, 1980), chap. 5, and "The Domestic Political Economy of Development," in Tim Niblock, ed., *State, Society and Economy in Saudi Arabia* (New York, 1982), p. 211.

b. Figure for 1966.

c. From table 2.

Another study, which classifies occupations by educational requirements (none, primary, secondary, etc.) rather than by function (bureaucrat, teacher, farmer, etc.), suggests that those pursuing occupations requiring at least a post-secondary modern education will number almost 170,000, that is, about 11 percent of a projected Saudi workforce of 1,563,000 by the middle of this decade.[4]

An even more significant indicator of the new middle class's salience may be its proportion of the urban, that is, nonagricultural, labor force. The total number of agricultural workers in Saudi Arabia is expected to be 584,400 in 1985.[5] The share of Saudi nationals in the agricultural labor force in 1975 was estimated at about 90 percent.[6] If we assume that this percentage remains substantially unchanged in 1985, then about 526,000 Saudi nationals will be engaged in agriculture. This total, if subtracted from the total projected Saudi labor force in table 3 of 1,379,500, would produce a nonagricultural labor force of about 853,500. Of this most politically relevant sub-population, the new middle class of 113,200 will account for over 13 percent.

Regardless of the measure chosen, the emergence of the new middle class as a substantial factor in Saudi society is undeniable. Furthermore, there is every indication that this class will continue to grow more quickly than the general Saudi population. While the political implications of this fact may not be self-evident, a comparison of Saudi Arabia's new middle class with that of other Arab countries is highly suggestive.

Table 4 classifies new middle class occupations by educational requirements rather than function, but the figure for the new middle class as a
percentage of total labor force in 1975—4.5 percent—is almost identical
to that in table 3, and the two classification schemes can therefore be taken
to be compatible. Table 4 reveals that in 1975, the new middle class was
already as salient in Saudi Arabia as it was in Syria and South Yemen.
However, Syria had experienced new middle class upheaval as long ago
as 1949, and its traditional elites were permanently ousted in 1963. In the
Popular Democratic Republic of Yemen (South Yemen), radical forces led
by elements of the new middle class had seized control of the nationalist
movement before independence and had taken the reins of government
when the British departed in 1968. Even more astonishing is the case of
Egypt, which was the first Arab state exposed to forces of social modernization. In 1975 Egypt's new middle class was only twice as weighty as Saudi
Arabia's. But Egypt underwent its political upheaval and regime transformation more than thirty years ago, when its new middle class was almost
certainly much smaller, in proportional terms, than Saudi Arabia's in 1975.

**Table 4. Labor force by occupational level and educational attainment, 1975
(in thousands)**

Group	Saudi Arabia	Syria	PDRY	Egypt
Professional and technical (science- and math-based university degrees)	6.0	16.1	0.8	168.7
Other professional (liberal- and fine arts-based university degrees)	17.9	25.7	1.0	267.5
Sub-professional/ technical (1–3 year science- and math-based secondary or vocational secondary degrees)	5.3	11.2	1.4	228.7
Other sub-professional (1–3 year nonscience- and math-based post-secondary or vocational secondary degrees)	28.7	35.2	1.1	255.0
Subtotal (new middle class)	57.9	88.2	4.3	919.9
Total labor force	1,298.2	1,741.0	88.8	9,070.2
New middle class as % of labor force	4.5	5.1	4.8	10.1

Source: I. Serageldin et al., "Manpower and International Labor Migration
in the Middle East and North Africa," in The World Bank, Technical Assistance
and Special Studies Division, *Final Report* (June 1981), table 4.8, p. 75, table 4.10,
p. 77, and table 5.4, p. 179.

It is therefore clear that the new middle class in Saudi Arabia has attained a "critical mass" that, in other countries, has produced revolutionary change. It is less clear that Saudi Arabia is condemned by history to conform to the pattern of these other countries. Saudi Arabia may be a special case, the beneficiary of so many unique advantages that it can avoid a major rift between the regime and the new middle class. Or this rift may simply be delayed by a developmental time lag, meaning that Saudi Arabia's "immunity" to the new middle class "disease" is only temporary. These issues will be explored in greater detail in the next section.

4. THE NEW MIDDLE CLASS AS A DISSIDENT FORCE IN SAUDI POLITICS

The analysis thus far has elaborated a model of the revolutionary role of the new middle class, has demonstrated its operation in analogous societies, and has documented the rise of the new middle class in Saudi Arabia. The operational question now becomes: to what extent is this model likely to be applicable to Saudi Arabia within a mid-range time frame of, say, two to ten years?

In dealing with this question it might be useful to glance at the historical record for telltale indications of new middle class restlessness or subversive activity and then go on to assess the peculiar circumstances of Saudi Arabia that may mitigate or aggravate the operability of the model in its particular case.

Historical Glimpse

Saudi Arabia is a closed political system, and the regime has been particularly anxious to suppress information about political unrest and subversive activity. Nevertheless, enough evidence has seeped out over the years to suggest that a considerable amount of unrest has manifested itself among the new middle class in both the military and civilian sectors.

The first known instance of subversive activity among military officers occurred in 1955, when a group of "Free Officers" modeled on the Egyptian prototype was uncovered. In 1962 the defection of air force pilots to Egypt during the Egyptian-Saudi confrontation stemming from the Yemen civil war led to the grounding of the entire air force. Declassified intelligence from that period estimated that most of the forty-odd air force officers were secret sympathizers with Gamal Abdul Nasser. The most serious instances of unrest among the military cited in many open sources are the abortive coup attempts of June and September 1969, which led to waves of arrests and purges of civilians as well as military personnel. The measures taken to deal with suspected and actual disloyalty in the armed forces have typically had the effect of impairing military modernization and professionalization. It is known, for instance, that until the early 1970s, Hijazis were discriminated against in recruitment to the armed forces and in promotions into the officer corps because their loyalty was in doubt, setting back programs for national defense based on the development of the armed forces. Since then, the regime has apparently tried to reduce the risks of discontent by lavishing high pay and benefits on the military. Yet there has been at least one confirmed report of an aborted coup in 1977 in addition to several cases of defections of individuals and small groups of officers. In the civilian sector, clandestine and exiled new middle class political movements have made their existence known through their own propaganda, but their size and the extent of their support are difficult to determine. The best known of these have been the Saudi Liberation Front, a Nasserist organization, and the Union of the People of the Arabian Peninsula, led by Nasir al-Sa'id.

However, the extent of the existence of new middle class political pressure on the regime can perhaps best be inferred from the constant revival of the Basic Law issue. Ever since the death of King Abd al-Aziz, each time the regime appeared to be experiencing difficulties at home or abroad or undergoing a succession, the rulers felt it necessary to assuage a perceived pressure by promising a Basic Law that would define the rights and obligations of citizens while expanding and regulating their participation in the political process. That was the case in 1958 (the Saud-Faisal struggle), 1960 (the same), 1962 (domestic turmoil and the Yemen war), 1970 (in the wake of the 1969 coup attempts and purges), 1975 (Faisal's assassination), 1979 (the takeover of the Grand Mosque in Mecca and external crises), and 1982 (Khaled's death). Each time, the immediate crisis passed, the promise was shelved, only to be reiterated during the next crisis, a clear reflection of the rulers' sense of a pent-up demand for the kind of legal-rational charter or constitution typically aspired to by the new middle class.

Peculiar Saudi Circumstances

The historical glimpse points out that the new middle class has already become problematic in Saudi Arabia. However, even this brief overview of new middle class restlessness suggests the existence of factors peculiar to Saudi Arabia that may affect the applicability to it of the general conceptual model of new middle class behavior.

In the military sector, for example, it is noteworthy that most of the instances of military unrest took place before 1970, when regional politics were dominated by the drive for integral Arab unity led by Nasser and sustained by his appeal even after the setback he suffered in 1967. The decline of Arab nationalist emotion since his death has greatly reduced that source of pressure on the monarchy as well as on other polities in the region. Syria and Iraq, for instance, which had experienced frequent regime turnovers in the 1950s and 1960s, have had the same regimes since 1970. Jordan, too, after dealing with its upheaval in 1970–71, has experienced remarkably little domestic turmoil.

On the other hand, Saudi Arabia has experienced at least one known attempt at a military coup in 1977. Moreover, the massive military build-up since 1973 may have made it more difficult than ever for the kingdom to insulate itself from other potentially disruptive regional developments, such as the Arab-Israeli conflict, even as it may have enhanced the weight and position of the military within the political system. In this respect, the inclusion of military officers in Saudi discussions with U.S. Secretary of Defense Weinberger in 1982 (for the first time as far as is known) may be ominous. It suggests that the Saudi authorities have begun to find it necessary to involve the military in foreign policy decision making, which in turn may mean trouble in case of disagreement and policy failure.

In the civilian sector, the fact that the regime has successfully withheld a Basic Law indicates that new middle class pressure has not yet become irresistible. However, the repeated failures to deliver after promises had been made betray serious divisions within the royal family on this issue. These differences manifested themselves during the 1960s in the context of the power struggle among Saud, Faisal, and the Free Princes, and of the Saudi-Egyptian confrontation over Yemen. A similar split over the issue in the future would prove more damaging to the regime than in the past. On the other hand, suppression of the issue for the sake of preserving family unity might well impair the regime's ability to make adaptations necessary for its survival.

The ambiguity of the historical record makes it all the more necessary to undertake an investigation of factors peculiar to Saudi Arabia that might mitigate or enhance the applicability of the new middle class model, before attempting any final conclusions. Three such factors stand out: the country's immense wealth; the size and role of the royal family; and vastness of territory and lack of structural integration.

On the face of it, these factors appear to make a new middle class revolt both less probable and less likely to succeed if it were attempted. However, on closer examination it appears that those same factors involve elements that make the model even more applicable. The balance between the two sets of elements does not always favor regime maintenance.

Wealth. Oil revenues have been the lubricant of the Saudi entity. Huge financial surpluses have mitigated the strains of development and provided a safety net for inefficiencies and mistakes. In particular, they have given the regime the wherewithal to satisfy the material demands and expectations of all segments of Saudi society, including the new middle class, and thereby to moderate the competition for resources that has frequently led to the downfall of regimes in other modernizing countries. Saudi Arabia's unique position as the world's largest oil exporter and possessor of the world's largest recoverable oil reserves has held out the prospect of freedom from economic constraint, with all its political ramifications. Throughout the 1970s, it did seem that Saudi Arabia would be able to count on its ability to deflect middle class aspirations in the direction of economic self-gratification.

However, Saudi wealth, though justifiably envied by other modernizing regimes, is no guarantee against future social and political dislocations. Three separate, albeit related, problems cast doubt on the extent to which this wealth will exempt Saudi Arabia from developmental stresses.

The first of these is the problem of distribution, not just in the technical sense but in terms of the normative principles underlying patterns of resource distribution. In all societies experiencing rapid economic growth, the overall absolute improvement in living standards initially tends to overshadow the question of relative distribution and contributes to social peace. Eventually, however, people cease to measure their positions against their own previous levels and look instead at their share relative to that of other elements in society. Because different social groups invariably undergo differential rates of economic improvement, a sense of deprivation generally emerges among the relatively less favored groups regardless of the performance of the economy as a whole. In the case of Saudi Arabia, this problem may assume a more severe expression than elsewhere because of the large size of the royal family.

If grievances cast in relative terms emerge, it is very difficult to redress them except by a conscious political decision to reorder the basis of social stratification; this would go to the very heart of the Saudi monarchical system. Piecemeal, preemptive reform, of the kind undertaken so far by Saudi Arabia, might alleviate the problem temporarily; but the historical record of other regimes faced with similar dilemmas is not encouraging for the somewhat longer term. Comparative studies of revolution, including those by de Tocqueville, have indicated that traditional regimes are in greatest danger not when they stick to their principles but precisely when they begin to reform.

A second wealth-related problem for Saudi Arabia concerns the source of that wealth. Saudi prosperity has depended almost exclusively on oil, hence, on the vagaries of the world oil market. For much of the past decade, that market appeared to promise ever increasing revenues, but more recent changes have tarnished the glow of Saudi Arabia's economic prospects. Because of reduced world demand and increased production by new exporters, both the price of oil and Saudi market share declined perceptibly after 1979. In January 1983 Saudi production had dropped from a peak of more than 10 million barrels per day (mbd) in 1980 to about 4 mbd.[8]

At the official posted price of $29 per barrel, adopted by OPEC in March 1983, the income generated from this level of production (about $53 billion per year) would fall far short of the $72.5 billion per year needed to fulfill the development, defense, and aid programs of the Third Five Year Plan.[9] Unless this situation is reversed before too long, deep cuts will have to be made in projected expenditures, and this could result in disappointed hopes with potentially dangerous political reverberations.

Some of the factors that have clouded Saudi Arabia's economic prospects are probably transitory. An end to the world economic recession, perhaps facilitated by lower oil prices, would stimulate demand for oil. Other producers, notably Britain, will cease to be exporters when their modest reserves are depleted in a few years. However, part of the change in demand patterns is structural. Conservation measures (energy efficient equipment, insulation) will not be reversed. Furthermore, some exporters, especially Iraq, are now out of the market because of physical constraints but will return to it when these constraints are removed.

It is, of course, impossible to predict with certainty what Saudi revenues will be in the coming years, but Saudi Arabia remains vulnerable to market forces beyond its own control, and it is possible that Saudi assumptions about those forces have been overly optimistic and that Saudi planning has been excessively ambitious.

If that should prove to be the case and a major funds-flow problem were to emerge, the result might be viewed as a monumental regime failure, producing bitter recriminations and mutual accusations among the regime and the new middle class, the conservatives and the modernizers, and other important social formations. In short, a crisis precisely of the type postulated by the new middle class model might result.

Saudi rulers could attempt to moderate the impact of reduced revenues for a while by drawing on financial reserves and overseas investments, which are currently equivalent to almost two years of projected expenditures. If the problem persists, some more painful adjustments would be necessary, in the form of program cutbacks or "stretch-outs," and these would entail system-wide strains centering around the relative burden to be borne by different groups or programs in the overall budget. Intensified competition between different components of the armed forces for constant or diminishing government expenditures would be particularly ominous. It is noteworthy that a similar problem occurred, on a much smaller scale, in 1958, when drastic cutbacks decreed by Prince Faisal in response to the overspending of King Saud produced widespread resentment among the affected groups, including members of the royal family. Even if the ruling elite were able to agree on the specifics of retrenchment, there is no doubt that a palpable slowdown in the pace of development would dramatically reduce employment and promotion prospects for new middle class workers.

A third consideration is that even if Saudi oil revenues do not fall far below the expectations of the Third Plan, it is possible that employment opportunities for the new middle class may become a problem in the 1980s, simply because of the massive investment already made by the state in higher education. As table 5 indicates, there was a dramatic increase in the number of students at secular Saudi universities during the 1970s; by 1979–80, the figure exceeded 35,000. Furthermore, large numbers of Saudis—15,000 in 1980, according to one source—went to study abroad, where they acquired, usually at government expense, technical skills and perhaps some "dangerous" political and social ideas, as well.[10] Many of these graduates believe that they are entitled to prestigious and remunerative posts in the state sector, and during the period of the Third Plan (1981–85) they will be joined by 42,000 others who are expected to complete their studies with skills appropriate to professional and technical or sub-professional and sub-technical occupations.[11]

Table 5. Students in secular Saudi universities

University	1969–70	1971–72	1973–74	1975–76	1977–78	1979–80
University of Riyadh	2,899	3,782	5,567	7,807	10,500	13,124
King Abd al-Aziz University	265	1,976	3,939	9,986	19,949	19,287
University of Petroleum and Minerals (Dhahran)	450	723	1,240	1,716	1,616	2,794
Total	3,614	6,481	10,746	19,509	32,065	35,205

Source: Kingdom of Saudi Arabia, *Statistical Yearbook* (various years).

However, an examination of Saudi projections reveals that the total number of mid-grade civil service positions will increase by only 21,600 during this period, while new teaching posts may number only 12,500.[12] Even if all these 34,100 new openings are filled by Saudi nationals, there is still a distinct possibility that Saudi Arabia may face an oversupply of mid-level technical and professional workers.

At present, there is a shortage of Saudi nationals able or willing to fill all the positions created by the economic development programs. This has resulted in a heavy reliance on foreign workers in all sectors of the economy. Saudi Arabia's need for unskilled and semi-skilled imported labor will probably continue for the forseeable future, but the massive investment already made in higher education suggests that by the mid-1980s, Saudi Arabia may confront a novel problem of excess high-quality manpower. If such a situation were to occur, Saudi graduates could well be forced to take positions for which they were subjectively overqualified, and expressions of discontent could ensue unless other outlets for their skills and ambitions are found.

In general, any problem of surplus middle-class manpower in Saudi Arabia is unlikely to be critical provided a serious, prolonged decline in oil revenues does not take place. However, even if Saudi Arabia experiences nothing more disruptive than a slowdown in its rate of economic growth, the previously mentioned problems relating to the character and source of its wealth indicate that that asset alone does not suffice to make Saudi Arabia invulnerable to the strains normally associated with development and modernization.

The royal family. There are, by various estimates, between 3,000 and 5,000 male members in the different branches of the Al Saud family. The senior princes dominate the central and provincial governments; the junior princes occupy many posts in the upper ranks of the civil service, the quasi-governmental agencies and corporations, the armed forces, and large-scale private business.

In principle, the size of the royal family and its ubiquity in Saudi life provide a formidable defense for the regime. Potential plotters must reckon that some members would survive any coup and would try to restore the dynasty's fortunes with help from outside sources. This complicates the planning of coups and thus helps to deter them. Moreover, Saudi princes, located as they are in every important institution in the country, constitute an invaluable source of political intelligence. Many of them are highly qualified and competent individuals, whose contributions improve the overall performance of the regime. In these and other respects, the Saudi royal family is a potential asset not available to other modernizing regimes, monarchical or republican.

At the same time, the royal family is a potential liability of major proportions. Of those factors tending to reduce the political utility of the royal family, four merit particular attention.

The first of these, perhaps paradoxically, is the size of the family. In general, constantly increasing numbers of princes may help institutionalize a monarchical regime, but at some point of diminishing returns, continued growth makes control and cohesion difficult and is therefore counterproductive. While it is not obvious that this point has been reached in Saudi Arabia, it is likely that the princes will find it increasingly difficult, despite their obvious interest in repressing personal, ideological, clan, or generational conflicts, to maintain a façade of unity while their numbers grow, their interests diverge, and their traditional tribal origins recede further from living memory.

Furthermore, excessive size dilutes the "magical" aura of royalty and debases the status of the royal family to that of a mere privileged class or caste, perpetuating itself by arbitrary restrictions on marriage to commoners, especially for female members.

Second, royal family "activism" tends to exacerbate the structural tension between the traditional, ascriptive norms that underlie the privileged position of the princes and the universalistic, achievement-oriented values and aspirations of the large and growing new middle class.[13] These norms, which obstruct the professionalization and technical effectiveness of the armed forces, in particular, have a more general effect of clogging the channels of promotion for upwardly mobile commoners.

Resentment of inherited status may be especially pronounced in those branches of the public services—the technical ministries and armed forces—where appropriate qualifications are most evident and where the "career open to talent" is the ethos of those trained in the relevant disciplines. One of these branches is the air force, which has been disproportionately implicated in anti-regime conspiracies and which, perhaps not coincidentally, was the service least loyal to the shah of Iran.[14]

The resentment of entrenched royalty extends to the political sphere as well. Some commoners have achieved prominence and have been admitted to the higher levels of government by virtue of their technical expertise. A number of technical ministries (petroleum, planning, finance, communications, health) have long been held by technocrats, though even these are frequently affiliated with important clans. Commoners, however, continue to be excluded from the top positions in politically sensitive ministries, such as interior and defense. And those who have risen to high position owe their success to individual co-optation rather than to a routinized recruitment process; they function as councilors to the ranking princes, not as decision makers with independent authority. Furthermore, these senior technocrats are members of a very small group who acquired their training early on, when the rarity and marginal value of modern education were more pronounced and the political opportunities generated by this asset were correspondingly greater. As the new middle class continues to grow and more junior princes with modern education come of age, co-optation will become a progressively less satisfactory response to the aspirations of individual Saudis or the political norms of the class as a whole.

Third, the monarchy's viability depends, in part at least, on the collective reputation of the royal family. The Saudi princes are undoubtedly aware of their collective vulnerability and realize that their own unity is a major element in their survival. However, this awareness has not prevented some princes from behaving in ways (indulgence in corruption, conspicuous consumption, etc.) that bring discredit on the family as a whole.

Fourth, historically, the most glaring threat to regime unity has been the failure to regularize the succession process. Members of the royal family have engaged in serious and protracted struggles, one of the most significant features of which was the willingness of all parties involved to reach out for support beyond the family circle. Sometimes, this led to appeals to the new middle class, based on programs of constitutional or socioeconomic reforms; King Saud and the Free Princes promised a constitution in 1960, and Faisal did the same in 1962 along with other promises of reform in his famous ten-point program. "Foreign powers" have been enlisted in attempts to unseat rivals. The Free Princes, led by Talal ibn Abd al-Aziz, moved to Cairo after their break with King Saud, where they made common cause with the Saudi National Liberation Front and engaged in openly dissident political activities. In 1964, when King Saud himself lost out in the struggle with Faisal and was deposed, he was granted political asylum in Cairo and thereafter supported Nasser in his program to destabilize Saudi Arabia. The assassination of King Faisal by Prince Faisal ibn Musa'id in 1975 may have been due to a personal grievance, but the struggles of the 1950s and 1960s were definitely rooted in the ambiguities of the traditional concept of succession; these remain in force and are unlikely to be clarified.

Altogether, then, the character of the royal family may complicate the applicability of the new middle class model to Saudi Arabia, but it does not by any means invalidate it and in certain respects makes it even more relevant.

Territorial vastness and structure. In many developing societies, political and economic power, transportation and communications links, and cultural-national symbols are so centralized that it is sufficient to seize the "center," usually the capital city, in order to take control of the entire system. Saudi Arabia does not fit this pattern. Power resides in the royal family rather than in a place. The family itself is dispersed, along with religious and cultural symbols and military commands, throughout different parts of the country that are still somewhat unintegrated. This makes Saudi Arabia less vulnerable than other modernizing states to a revolutionary conspiracy.

However, since the massive increase in oil revenues and the adoption of vast development plans fueled by these revenues, the Saudi entity has come to depend more than ever before on a single economic center, the oil-producing Hasa region, and within that on a very small bottleneck around Ras Tanura, where the oil lines come to a head. If rebels were somehow to seize this area, they could hold the entire state hostage at least as effectively as could rebels in another case seizing the capital. The rebels would be in a position to extract far-reaching reforms from the regime or to overthrow the monarchy completely. Once more, because of the centrality of oil to Saudi Arabia, the structural "disconnectedness" of the country modifies but does not in itself make the new middle class model irrelevant.

This review of special Saudi circumstances has demonstrated that, insofar as the relevance of the new middle class model is concerned, Saudi peculiarities do not make that country exceptional. Indeed, it may be argued that, far from leaving Saudi Arabia exempt from the problem of new middle class alienation, circumstances tend on balance to aggravate the problem. It is therefore quite probable that the Saudi new middle class will soon enter the third stage of historical evolution outlined in the conceptual model, if it has not already done so, and that the question remaining is whether some major crisis will arise in the period under consideration (the next ten years) to trigger an actual revolt of the new middle class. Such a crisis might well provoke an open and perhaps fatal split within the royal family. It would certainly demolish the regime's reputation for success in preserving the country's prosperity and security against outside dangers, which has thus far been a major factor in its hold on power.

5. POSSIBLE TRIGGERS OF A NEW MIDDLE CLASS REVOLT

The question of Saudi prosperity has already been treated; it is necessary only to repeat that the economic issue is already a potential domestic trigger of crisis. Current oil production and the concomitant levels of revenue, if not raised within three to five years, may well cause a crisis for the new middle class that could lead to a political explosion in the country.

The external dimension is even less predictable. There is, however, a multitude of potentially critical flashpoints; if any one of these sets off a chain of events ending in an outright Saudi military defeat, the consequences for the regime could be devastating. Saudi leaders, aware of the risks of military embarrassment, have been extremely reluctant to commit their armed forces to combat, even when the highest interests of the state were threatened (as in Yemen after 1962), and Saudi forces have never been posted abroad except on "deterrence" or peacekeeping missions (as in Kuwait in 1961 or Lebanon in 1976). However, Saudi Arabia may itself become the target of offensive action by foreign powers, and though there is little likelihood that the country would be overrun, even local defeat could have severe repercussions.

Saudi Arabia has potential disputes with several of its neighbors. The most volatile of these may be in the southwest. North Yemen (Yemen Arab Republic) has never been fully reconciled to Saudi control of the Asir and Tihama regions and has resented the Saudi hold on its northern tribes since 1962. South Yemen (PDRY) is ideologically hostile to the Saudi regime and shares a long, undemarcated boundary with Saudi Arabia that could flare up again, as it did in 1969, when PDRY incursions into Wadia forced the Saudis to send their regular army into battle. Either of the two Yemens could conceivably launch its forces against Saudi Arabia in support of territorial or other claims. Futhermore, the two Yemens continue to aspire to unity. If they were ever to merge, their combined forces could press Saudi defenses very hard indeed and perhaps seize control of Saudi Arabia's most important food-producing region.

Israel is even more capable of humiliating the Saudi military establishment. Israel has no direct claims on Saudi Arabia, but the persistence of the Arab-Israeli conflict could produce situations (a clash over navigation rights in the Gulf of Aqaba, domestic turmoil in Jordan resulting in competitive intervention by Israel and Saudi Arabia) with a potential for armed confrontation between the two states. Israel, moreover, appears to be concerned about the Saudi military build-up, especially in air power, that has taken place in recent years. A renewal of general Arab-Israeli warfare could lead Israel to preempt a perceived Saudi threat, whatever Saudi Arabia's actual intentions might be, by neutralizing the military facilities in the Tabuk region (which Israeli aircraft periodically overfly) and perhaps elsewhere in the kingdom.

The greatest threat, however, would appear to emanate from the northeast. The Iran-Iraq war has placed Saudi Arabia in an exceedingly uncomfortable position. Both belligerents have hegemonic aspirations in the Gulf and have military capacities that far outstrip Saudi Arabia's. If the war results in the defeat of one, there will be no regional power left to balance the other. An Iranian victory would be particularly dangerous in view of Saudi Arabia's past support for Iraq and the possible political ramifications among Saudi Shiites in the oil-bearing Eastern Province.

In a different sphere, an end to the war or even a stalemate or tacit agreement by the belligerents to confine themselves to low-level, localized combat would permit them to step up oil exports to finance their rearmament and economic rehabilitation. Although Iran was pumping at least 5 mbd before the pre-1979 turmoil, it may not want, for ideological reasons, to produce much above the level of about 3 mbd it had reached in January 1983. But Iraq, which has been exporting less than 1 mbd since the outbreak of the war, could increase that by 2–2.5 mbd if war-related constraints on production and transportation were alleviated. Without a simultaneous rise in world demand, Saudi Arabia would be forced to accept either a smaller market share or lower prices, that is, a major decline in oil revenues that would be only partly compensated by reduced economic assistance to Iraq. This could produce severe economic difficulties at home that might trigger new middle class action.

However, prolongation of the war would also be undesirable. Aside from the cost of subsidizing Iraq's war effort, there is a danger that the war could spread either to one of the undeclared Saudi "protégés" (Kuwait, Bahrain, Qatar, the UAE) or directly to Saudi territory. In particular, there is a possibility that Iranian leaders, frustrated by Iraq's continued resistance and believing that only Saudi assistance makes it possible, might attempt to strike, by air or sea, at Saudi assets across the Gulf. If successful, they would not only damage the Saudi economy but would also expose the country's military weakness. The regime would then become vulnerable to the charges and challenges of inefficiency, inability to protect the country, and so on, that are typically leveled against traditional regimes by the new middle class in developing societies.

In the face of contingencies discussed, the regime would presumably fall back on its ostensible domestic guarantor of last resort, the National Guard. The guard is equipped on modern lines but still recruits mainly from certain select bedouin tribes, and its loyalty to the royal family is assumed to be firm. However, the reliability of the guard is not beyond question. Some observers believe that economic modernization and programs of sedentarization have eroded the traditional loyalties that reinforced the material links between the Al Saud and the tribes and have left only a cash nexus.[15] Bedouin dependency on royal largesse is still great, but the decline in affective ties may mean that the guard is not immune to dissident ideas though it may not yet be receptive to appeals from the new middle class. In any case, in the few instances in which the guard has been called upon to carry out its assigned missions, it has not been uniformly impressive. In late 1979 and early 1980, National Guard forces did suppress Shiite demonstrations in the Eastern Province with great severity. But during the takeover of the Grand Mosque in Mecca, they reportedly did not perform well, and some of the rebels were said to have been former guardsmen.[16] These facts may have something to do with the post-1979 reduction in force of the guard (app. B, table B.1).

In the face of insuperable domestic trouble, a beleaguered royal house may be forced to call for outside protection. While President Reagan has intimated that the United States would be willing to help, American ability to intervene effectively against domestic opponents of the regime is unclear. Moreover, even a successful American effort on behalf of the regime might further inflame nationalist resentment of the Al Saud. Such interventions in the past, like the British show of force on behalf of Egypt's Wafd party in 1943 and the American involvement in the 1953 counter-coup that restored the shah of Iran to power, have temporarily strengthened threatened traditional elites but tarred them with the brush of collusion with imperialism and weakened their legitimacy. Foreign support may therefore provide short-term solutions, and in the case of the Al Saud, this may be all that foreign protectors are interested in. But it is no long-term guarantee for a traditional regime that cannot by itself cope with the consequences of modernization.

6. CONCLUSION

In most developing societies the new middle class has played a major role in the overthrow of traditional regimes. Although that class is brought forth by traditional regimes seeking "defensive modernization," it inevitably becomes alienated from its creators when the latter restrain the drive for modernization as it encroaches upon areas affecting their prerogatives or the "ideological" underpinnings of their power. At that stage a major failure of the regime in the domestic or foreign spheres has acted as a trigger to revolution often executed by military officers—the armed component of the new middle class.

In Saudi Arabia a new middle class has emerged as a pivotal social formation and is bound to grow even more salient in the near future. It already showed signs of restlessness in the 1960s, but because of the play of mitigating circumstances, these were fewer in the 1970s.

Indications are that the general new middle class model applies to Saudi Arabia despite the existence of several seemingly countervailing factors peculiar to that country. Abundant wealth, a very large royal family, and a vast and disconnected territory proved under close investigation to have ambiguous, aggravating as well as mitigating, effects. While these factors may complicate the applicability of the model, they do not make Saudi Arabia a unique case, exempt from its operation.

Because an upheaval involving the new middle class depends on the trigger of a severe crisis, the time frame within which such an upheaval may take place in Saudi Arabia cannot be predicted with assurance. It is, however, clear that there are several sources of potentially severe crises in Saudi Arabia. The chances that one of these crises will erupt and produce upheaval within the next ten years are considerably greater than even.

27

Appendix A. Middle class civil servants in Saudi Arabia

The figures on mid-grade Saudi civil servants recalled in the text have
been derived from a variety of sources and are based on a number of assumptions used to distill the available information. The methodology of
producing these figures is essentially reductionist. Total government employment is taken as a base point. Table A.1 shows the growth in civilian
government employment since 1960, as reported in various years of the
Statistical Yearbook and includes a projection for 1985 derived from the Third
Development Plan (p. 99).

Table A.1. Civilian government employees, in and out of cadre (in thousands)

	1960	1965	1970	1975	1980	1985
Number	44	92	129	193	326	421
(% increase)		(109)	(40)	(50)	(69)	(29)

The figures in table A.1, however, include a substantial number of daily
wage workers who are not considered civil servants proper or members of
the new middle class. In-cadre employees—the true bureaucrats—are assigned grades from 1 (the lowest) to 15 (the highest before ministerial rank).
The growth in the number of government employees is depicted in table
A.2. These figures are also derived from the *Statistical Yearbook*.

Table A.2. In-cadre civilian government employees
(in thousands)

	1960	1965	1970	1975	1980
Number	22.9	53.4	76.8	135.2	245.4
(% increase)		(132)	(44)	(76)	(82)
In-cadre as % of all government employees	52.0	58.0	59.5	70.1	75.3

The number of in-cadre employees has clearly increased at a faster rate than that of all employees, but the corps of mid- and upper-grade civil servants has grown even faster. Grade 7 has been chosen as the mid-grade boundary in this study because it corresponds to the military rank of second lieutenant and it is assumed that those in grades 7 and above possess new middle class skills and education and perhaps perspectives as well. Table A.3 shows their progress since 1960.

Table A.3 Civilian government employees, grades 7–15 (in thousands)

	1960	1965	1970	1975	1980
Number	1.9	4.8	8.1	24.1	54.2
(% increase)		(150)	(66)	(200)	(125)
As % of all government employees	4.3	5.2	6.3	12.5	16.6

Projected growth. The official projected increase of about 95,000 in total government employment by 1985 (table A.1) is an aggregate figure, with no indication of the expected distribution among different categories. It is reasonable to assume, however, that in-cadre employment will continue to grow more rapidly than will out-cadre and that the grade 7–15 group, because of rising educational qualifications in the population, will experience the most rapid growth of all. If this category's share of total government employment should rise from 16.6 percent in 1980 to, say, 18 percent in 1985, the total number would reach 75,800, that is, an increase of 21,600 over 1980, or about 40 percent growth (compared to 29 percent for total government employment).

Saudi nationals. The figures used thus far are derived from official Saudi statistics. These do not distinguish between Saudi citizens and expatriates; some adjustment factor is necessary if the size of the civil service component of the new Saudi middle class is to be estimated.

Although Saudi nationals are generally assumed to account for about 55–60 percent of the overall service sector of the Saudi economy, the public bureaucracy is only a part of the entire service sector. In an effort to overcome this problem, the authors of a major study of Saudi employment patterns constructed a sub-category of the service sector— public administration, education, and health—of which civil servants are assumed to constitute the great majority. According to these calculations, Saudi nationals represented 75 percent of employees in this subsector in 1975 (Richard I. Lawless, "Country Case Study: Saudi Arabia," in J. S. Birks and C. A. Sinclair, *The International Migration Project*, University of Durham, 1978, table 23, p. 50). This would appear to be a reasonable adjustment factor to generate orders of magnitude, and if it is applied to the data in table A.3 and to the projection for mid-grade civil servants in 1985, the results in table A.4 are produced.

Table A.4. Estimate of Saudi nationals' share in total mid-grade civil service (in thousands)

	1965	1970	1975	1980	1985
Total employees, grades 7–15	4.8	8.1	24.1	54.2	75.8
Saudi nationals (75% of total)	3.6	6.0	18.1	40.7	56.8

It should be emphasized that these figures are only estimates and that the increasing availability of educated Saudis by 1985 may produce a larger proportion of Saudi nationals in the civil service.

Appendix B. Military Officers

Saudi military manpower includes both the regular armed forces and various para-military forces, of which the National Guard is by far the largest. Figures on manpower since the mid-1960s are derived from statistics in *The Military Balance*, published by the International Institute of Strategic Studies and presented in table B.1.

Table B.1 Military manpower in Saudi Arabia (in thousands)

Year	Regular armed forces	Para-military	Total
1967–68	36	20	56
1968–69	36	20	56
1969–70	34	108[a]	—
1970–71	36	24	60
1971–72	41	30	71
1972–73	40.5	10	50.5
1973–74	42.5	10	52.5
1974–75	43	32.5	75.5
1975–76	47	22.5	69.5
1976–77	51.5	26.5	78
1977–78	61.5	41.5	102
1978–79	58.5	41.5	99
1979–80	44.5	26.5	71
1980–81	47	26.5	73.5
1981–82	51.7	36.5	88.2

a. Includes people's militia (100,000) and gendarmerie (8,000). Since the basis for this estimate deviates so clearly from that of other years, total manpower has not been computed.

Projected growth. Projecting future growth is problematic simply because rates of change in the past have been so volatile. Political, budgetary, and manpower factors have all entered into force development. Changes in the size of the para-military forces have been particularly erratic, and in the absence of reasonable trend data, it has simply been assumed that by 1985 these will number 41,500, implying an increase of some 5,000 after 1981 in order to regain the level of 1977 and 1978.

The regular armed forces have grown at a steadier rate, which for the last two years in table B.1 averaged 7.8 percent. This rate, which appears to reflect Saudi priorities and intentions in the coming years, was applied to the 1982 figure to yield a projected size of 69,800 in 1985. Thus, the estimated combined manpower of military and para-military forces in 1985 is expected to be 111,300.

Officer corps. The officer corps has been assumed to comprise one-tenth of total manpower. This assumption produces the number of officers shown in table B.2.

Table B.2 Saudi military manpower and officer corps
(in thousands)

	1967	1970	1975	1980	1985
Armed forces	36	36	47	47	69.8
Para-military	20	24	22.5	26.5	41.5
Total manpower	56	60	69.5	73.5	111.3
Officers	5.6	6.0	7.0	7.4	11.1

Appendix C. Teachers

The number of teachers in Saudi Arabia has grown dramatically since 1960. The figures in table C.1, drawn from various issues of the *Statistical Yearbook*, show the breakdown by level and nationality.

These data indicate that the rates of increase have varied directly with the level of education, reflecting the time lag in the through-put of the different levels, and that the overall distribution by nationality has not changed significantly.

Projection. The Third Five Year Plan anticipates a 16 percent increase in the number of all teachers by 1985, that is, an increase of about 12,500. Although the plan also forecasts an (unspecified) increase in the proportion of Saudi nationals in the teaching corps, the consistency of distribution since 1960 would seem to justify a conservative assumption that Saudis in 1985 will still constitute no more than half of all teachers, that is, 45,300. A more rapid growth in the Saudi-national share of teaching posts may, however, be both possible and necessary.

Table C.1 Teachers in Saudi Arabia by level and nationality

Level	1960 S	1960 NS	1960 T	1965 S	1965 NS	1965 T	1970 S	1970 NS	1970 T	1975 S	1975 NS	1975 T	1980 S	1980 NS	1980 T
Elementary	2,078	1,997	4,075	4,762	4,575	9,337	8,251	7,927	16,178	18,147	11,609	29,756	30,128	15,976	46,104
(% increase)						(129)			(73)			(84)			(55)
Intermediate	173	271	444	558	874	1,432	1,282	2,004	3,286	2,348	5,091	7,439	3,744	12,698	16,442
(% increase)						(223)			(129)			(126)			(121)
Secondary	17	70	87	24	105	129	97	412	509	415	1,717	2,132	935	4,657	5,592
(% increase)						(48)			(294)			(319)			(162)
Higher	13	35	48	56	143	199	134	343	477	538	1,203	1,741	1,608	3,165	4,773
(% increase)						(316)			(140)			(265)			(174)
Other[b]	132	418	550	304	963	1,267	405	1,282	1,687	789	1,920	2,709	1,539	3,651	5,190
(% increase)						(130)			(33)			(61)			(92)
Total	2,413	2,791	5,204	5,704	6,660	12,364	10,169	11,968	22,137	22,237	21,540	43,777	37,954	40,147	78,101
(% increase)						(138)			(79)			(98)			(78)
(% by nationality)	46	54	100	46	54	100	46	54	100	51	49	100	49	51	100

a. S = Saudi; NS = non-Saudi; T = Total.

b. Teacher training, religious studies, special studies.

NOTES

1. John H. Kautsky, *The Political Consequences of Modernization* (New York, 1972), pp. 106–107.

2. Elie Kedourie, *Nationalism in Asia and Africa* (New York, 1970), pp. 80–81.

3. J. S. Birks and C. A. Sinclair, "The Domestic Political Economy of Development in Saudi Arabia," in Tim Niblock, ed., *State, Society and Economy in Saudi Arabia* (New York, 1982), p. 199.

4. See I. Serageldin et al., "Manpower and International Labor Migration in the Middle East and North Africa," in World Bank, Technical Assistance and Special Studies Division, *Final Report* (June 1981), table 4.10, p. 77.

5. Birks and Sinclair, "The Domestic Political Economy," table 11.3, p. 211.

6. Cited in Saad Eddin Ibrahim, *The New Arab Social Order: A Study of the Impact of Oil Wealth* (Boulder, Colo., 1982), table 5.1, p. 96.

7. See Adeed I. Dawisha, "Internal Values and External Threats: The Making of Saudi Foreign Policy," *Orbis* (Spring 1979), 134.

8. According to one report, Saudi production then was actually 4.2 mbd, less than was necessary to generate the natural gas that fuels Saudi utilities and water desalination plants. *New York Times*, January 24, 1983, and January 25, 1983.

9. Total spending in 1981–85 was projected at $363 billion. Birks and Sinclair, "The Domestic Political Economy," p. 209.

10. William B. Quandt, *Saudi Arabia in the 1980s: Foreign Policy, Security, and Oil* (Washington, 1981), p. 55n.

11. Serageldin et al., "Manpower and International Labor Migration," table 4.12, p. 87.

12. For civil growth, see app. A; for number of teachers, see app. C.

13. Manfred W. Wenner, "Saudi Arabia: Survival of Traditional Elites," in Frank Tachau, ed., *Political Elites and Political Development in the Middle East* (Cambridge, Mass., 1975), p. 176.

✗ 14. See Farhad Kazemi, "The Military and Politics in Iran: The Uneasy Symbiosis," in Elie Kedourie and Sylvia G. Haim, eds., *Towards a Modern Iran: Studies in Thought, Politics and Society* (London, 1980).

15. See Arnold Hottinger, "Political Institutions in Saudi Arabia, Kuwait and Bahrain," in Shahram Chubin, ed., *Security in the Persian Gulf,* vol. 1, *Domestic Political Factors* (Montclair, N.J., 1981), p. 17; also Shirley Kay, "Social Change in Modern Saudi Arabia," in Niblock, *State, Society and Economy,* p. 173, and Ibrahim, *The New Arab Social Order,* p. 8.

16. Ibid., p. 116. See also Jim Paul, "Insurrection at Mecca," *Merip Reports,* 91 (October 1980), 3–4; and Quandt, *Saudi Arabia,* p. 95n.